Body language and communication
A guide for people with autism spectrum disorders

Simon Perks
Illustrated by Steve Lockett

First published 2007 by The National Autistic Society
393 City Road, London EC1V 1NG
www.autism.org.uk

ISBN 978 1 905722 29 7

Printed by Crowes

Contents

Introduction

When it comes to social interaction, people communicate using much more than words. Our eyes, our facial expressions, how we stand and what gestures we make all help to show how we feel and what we are trying to say.

For people with autism spectrum disorders, this 'body language' can appear just as foreign as if people were speaking ancient Greek. This means that we miss out on many of the things that people are trying to convey to us and can ourselves send mixed signals when the words we use are not consistent with what our body is saying.

I have based this book on my own experiences as someone with Asperger syndrome. For many years, I found it very difficult to communicate with people and often wondered whether there was some secret social language spoken by everybody but me. It turns out that I was almost right. There is another language, but it is not a spoken one.

However, just as we can learn French or German, we can also learn body language. In this book, we will learn how we can use simple body language techniques to interact more successfully and more enjoyably with our families, our friends, our colleagues and the many other people we meet each day.

We will look first at some of the key aspects of social interaction, such as meeting people, starting conversations, speaking and listening. In each case, we will look at how we can use body language to recognise how other people are feeling and to help us to communicate with them positively and with confidence.

We will then turn our attention to applying these skills in practice, firstly in conversations with individuals and then with larger groups and at social events. We will also consider what body language we can use when we encounter an unfamiliar situation and are not sure what to do.

As this book is based on my own experiences, it reflects my own cultural and social background, such as the people I meet and the things I do. However, we are all different, so what works for me may not automatically be right for you. When thinking about the ideas in this book, I would encourage you to think about how you can relate them to your own experiences and apply them to your own ways of living, working and socialising. To help you do this, we will conclude this book by discussing how we can develop our body language skills further and what resources are available to us.

By learning and using the basic 'grammar' and 'vocabulary' of body language, I have found that I am able to interact more enjoyably and more effectively with other people and to develop more rewarding social and professional relationships. In writing this book, I hope that it will help you to do the same.

Meeting and greeting people

We meet people every day. Some of them will be people we know well, such as our families, friends and work colleagues, while others will be people we know only vaguely or not at all. Each time we meet someone, it is important that we make the right impression. However, this is most important when we meet someone for the first time.

Making first impressions count

In his book *Body language*, Gordon Wainwright suggests that many people make up their minds about somebody within the first five minutes of meeting them. In order to do this, they use the information that they have in front of them – what we look like, what we say and how we behave. They use this information to form an assumption of what we are like, or the type of person we are. Once they have formed this opinion, it takes a lot for them to change it. This is why people say that 'first impressions count'.

In general, when we meet someone, we want him or her to like us. We all like people who are friendly, open and confident, so we need to make sure that we come across like this when we meet people. It is our body language that can help us to do this.

Having a friendly face

The first thing that people look at when they meet someone is his or her face. In particular, they tend to look at the other person's eyes. Consequently, eye contact is one of the most powerful elements of body language. When meeting someone, it is important that we make and maintain eye contact, at least until the initial introductions are over. It shows that we are interested in them and that they have our full attention.

Make eye contact when meeting people and smile.

People may think that we are not pleased to see them if we do not make eye contact or smile.

It is also important to smile. We smile when we are happy, and when we are not happy we do not smile. When we meet people, we want them to know that we are glad to see them, and we can convey this message by smiling when we greet them.

The good thing about a smile is that it is contagious – when we smile at someone, they tend to smile back automatically. This makes them feel more positive about meeting us. If we greet someone without smiling, they can think that we are not pleased to see them. This makes it much more difficult for us to make a good first impression.

It is useful to note that a genuine smile doesn't only affect the mouth, but also produces wrinkles around the eyes. If people 'force' an insincere smile, their mouth smiles but their eyes stay the same. So if someone is smiling at you with their mouth but not with their eyes, it can be a sign that they are not really happy to see you or that they are only trying to be polite. It could also mean that they are feeling unhappy, in which case the absence of a genuine smile is no reflection on us. Although it may seem to be a subtle difference, people will usually pick up on this and respond to it automatically. If we meet someone and our smile is not genuine then people may think that we are not pleased to see them. They may even ask if we are alright, because they think we may be feeling sad.

Adopting a confident stance

When we meet someone, we should give him or her our full and undivided attention. To greet someone while doing something else, such as watching television or typing on a computer, can be seen as very rude.

So in general, when we meet someone it is polite to stop what we are doing and take the time to greet him or her. This may seem inconvenient, particularly if we are doing something important, but stopping what we are doing can be seen by the person we are meeting as a sign that we think that meeting them is also important.

One way in which we can indicate that someone has our full attention is through our body position and posture. Firstly, when meeting someone we should, if possible, stand up and make sure that there are no physical barriers between them and us. This puts both them and us on an equal footing, and stops us getting distracted by other things such as the work on our desk.

Secondly, we should make sure that we are standing close to the person we are meeting. However, it is also important not to stand too close. Everybody has their own 'personal space', which extends about one metre (one arm's length) around them. If other people enter this personal space, it can make the person feel uncomfortable or even threatened. Therefore, when meeting people we should try to stand about one to one-and-a-half metres in front of them. This means that we are not entering their personal space, but that we are able to engage with them comfortably.

We should stand quite close to people we meet...

...but not too close.

Thirdly, we should face the person that we are meeting. This means that we should make sure that our entire body (our head, our torso and our feet) is oriented towards that person. This demonstrates that he or she has our full attention.

Making positive gestures

What we do when we meet someone depends on how well we know him or her. When I meet my sister, for example, I give her a hug. But I would not hug my boss or my bank manager.

When we meet someone for the first time, it is usual to shake his or her hand. Some people read a lot about us from how we shake hands, so it is something that it is worth getting right.

A handshake should be a positive greeting. But when we are meeting new people, this can make us nervous, which in turn can make our palms cold and clammy. People do not like a cold, clammy handshake, so it is always best to try to make sure our palms are dry before we meet someone. If necessary, and if you have time, you could dry them in the nearest washroom or (subtly) on a handkerchief. This is possible if you know in advance that you are meeting someone or that someone is coming to meet you. If the meeting is unplanned, don't go to the washroom when you see the other person approaching, as to make someone wait for you like this would be seen as rude. In such circumstances, the best thing to do is simply to not worry about your hands and to focus on greeting the other person.

When we meet someone, he or she may offer their hand first. If they do not, we can offer our own hand for them to shake. When shaking hands, keep your palm vertical and use the same amount of pressure as the other person. If you use too little pressure, the other person may think that you are weak or submissive, whereas if you use too much pressure, they may find you rude and aggressive. Bear in mind, however, that people may have a weaker handshake for other reasons, for example because of their age or because they have hurt their hand or arm.

As we shake someone's hand, it is normal to maintain eye contact. We can also use this opportunity to offer a few words of greeting, to reinforce the positive message that we are trying to give. I usually say something like 'pleased to meet you' or 'nice to meet you at last'.

You may find it useful to practise shaking hands with someone that you trust, who can tell you if you are using the right amount of pressure.

You may have noticed that some people use hugs or kisses when they greet each other. This is most common with family members or close friends, rather than with people we do not know. While it is perfectly acceptable to hug a family member or kiss them on the cheek, it is usually not appropriate to do so with someone we do not know that well. Because an inappropriate greeting can cause a great deal of offence, it is best not to hug or kiss people who are not close family members unless they do so first.

Another thing to note is that people from different cultures may greet each other in different ways. For example, in some cultures it may be common to hug or kiss someone when meeting them, even if for the first time. In others, people may not make physical contact at all. If we are not sure how to greet someone, a useful rule is to wait and see how he or she greets us and then to do the same.

Summary: making a good first impression

- make eye contact

- smile

- give the person your full attention

- do not stand too close

- shake hands

- say something like 'I'm pleased to meet you'.

Seeing someone we know

We have focused so far on meeting someone for the first time. However, we will also often meet people that we already know, such as friends and work colleagues. As these people already know us, it is less important for us to concentrate on making a good first impression, but it is still important for us to come across as friendly, open and confident.

As before, the first thing we should do is make eye contact with the other person. We can do this wherever we meet them, whether it is in the street, at work, in the pub or at college or university. However, we do not need to shake their hand each time we see them, so a less formal manner of greeting is often appropriate.

When the person looks at us, we can show that we have seen and recognised them by moving our eyebrows up and down quickly once. This 'eyebrow flash' acts as a kind of informal greeting, and is particularly effective if accompanied by a smile (see pictures on right).

If someone greets us in this way, we should make the same gesture back. If the person maintains eye contact, they may wish to start a conversation. They may say hello to us, or we can say hello and ask them how they are. Conversely, if the person does not maintain eye contact, then they probably do not wish to engage in conversation with us, so it is perhaps best to continue with whatever we were doing.

An 'eyebrow flash' is a useful, informal greeting; it lets people know we have seen them.

People may not realise we have seen them if our facial expression doesn't change.

If we see someone that we know, but he or she is too far away for an 'eyebrow flash' to be seen, it is still polite to acknowledge him or her in some way. If we are outside or in a busy room, we could wave at them briefly – just raising one hand in a wave at shoulder height should be sufficient. Sometimes, however, this may not be appropriate. For example, if we are in a formal setting such as a lecture theatre, it may be better to greet the person by giving a single nod of our head and smiling. This shows that we have seen the person, but does not distract other people around us.

It seems very complicated to have all these different ways of greeting people, and it is sometimes tempting to ignore people rather than try to decide how best to greet them. However, we need to remember that if we see someone we know and do not greet them, that person can feel insulted that we have ignored them. Therefore, we should always make the effort to greet people we know.

Summary: seeing someone we know

- always acknowledge people you know
- make eye contact
- smile
- use the 'eyebrow flash' if they are near enough to see this
- say hello if the person maintains eye contact
- nod or wave if the person is further away.

Starting a conversation

Starting a conversation with someone can be an intimidating and awkward experience. Sometimes people want to talk to us, but we do not know how to start the conversation. Sometimes people do not want to talk to us, but we do not realise it. And sometimes we want to talk with someone but do not know what to say.

Fortunately, people's body language says a lot about what they are thinking. This means that if we pay attention to how people are standing, where they are looking and what they are doing, we can engage in conversation with them more confidently and more successfully.

Making contact

The key to starting a conversation is eye contact. We use eye contact to establish a link with someone, much like a computer uses a modem to establish a connection to the internet. And just like the internet, once that initial connection is established, communication becomes much easier.

Once we have made eye contact, we can acknowledge someone by using the 'eyebrow flash' and smiling. To start a conversation with someone, we need to be reasonably close to them, but we must not enter their personal space. It is best to aim to be about a metre-and-a-half away from the person, so we may need to walk over to them before speaking.

It is best not to approach people from behind, as it can frighten them if they do not know we are there. And if we approach people from directly in front of them, it can come across as aggressive, so it is perhaps best to approach them from the side or from diagonally ahead of them. This may involve making a small detour to get to the person we want to talk to, but it avoids surprising them and also gives us time to gauge their body language as we approach.

When we reach the person we want to talk to, it is often difficult to know where to stand. It may seem logical to stand directly in front of him or her, but this can be a little overbearing for the person we are talking to and can make them feel intimidated. Therefore, it is better to stand in front of the other person and slightly to one side. This will make the person feel more comfortable, and hopefully more inclined to talk to us.

If the person we want to talk to is sitting at a desk, however, then we can usually stand in front of their desk without worrying about intimidating them – this is because the desk forms a kind of 'barrier' between them and us. If we cannot stand in front of their desk (for example, because it is positioned against a wall or another desk), then we can stand to one side of it or even next to the person we want to talk to. In such circumstances, the person will usually turn to face us.

If we are taller than the person we want to talk to, we should be careful not to stand so close to them that we make them feel anxious or threatened. This is particularly important if we are standing up and the person we want to talk to is sitting down. We can avoid making the other person feel intimidated either by standing a bit further away from them so that we don't appear so tall, or by sitting down.

If we are already sitting next to the person we want to talk to, it is a little easier. As long as they are not busy doing something else, such as talking to the person on the other side of them, we can try to get their attention by leaning forward a little bit (so that they can see us), turning towards them (by turning our torso slightly in their direction and our head about 45 degrees towards them) and trying to make eye contact with them.

Saying the first words

Having indicated to the person through eye contact, our facial expression and our position that we would like to speak with them, we now need to say something. This can be quite daunting, and it is easy to worry about what to say. In my experience, the best thing to say first is simply 'hello' or 'hi'. We can then follow this up with a simple question (see page 20 for some ideas), which will hopefully draw the person into conversation.

Once we have asked a question, we should show that we are interested in the person's answer. We can do this by making eye contact with them and leaning our head to one side. This is something that people often do when they are listening, and shows that we are waiting for the other person to respond. Do not forget to listen to what the other person says – this is vital if we want our initial question to develop into a conversation.

Getting a positive response

We have considered how we can use eye contact, our facial expression, the position of our body, a brief greeting and a question to indicate that we would like to start a conversation with someone. But how do we know if they want to talk with us?

Basically, if we are trying to start a conversation with someone and they are happy to speak with us, they will 'mirror' the things that we do. For example, if we make eye contact with them, then they will make eye contact back. If we smile at them, they will smile at us.

When we are standing or sitting next to the person we want to talk to, they will probably turn towards us when they realise that we are trying to start a conversation with them. When we speak with them or ask them a question, someone who wants to speak with us will respond by answering our question and perhaps asking a question of their own.

Recognising when to leave someone alone

Sometimes, however, someone will not want to talk with us. This could be because they are speaking with someone else, because they are very busy or because they just do not feel like talking. In such cases, we should not interrupt the other person. The thing to remember is that, if someone does not want to talk with us, it probably is not because of anything we have said or done. People sometimes just do not want to talk, and we need to accept that.

If someone does not want to talk with us, they will probably not make eye contact with us or may make eye contact for only a brief period. They will probably also face away from us, with their head, their torso and their feet. If we ask him or her a question, they will probably give us only a very brief or terse reply, and may not respond at all.

In such circumstances, it is probably best to stop trying to speak with the person. We could say something like 'anyway, nice to see you' and then walk away. This is not because we have 'failed' in trying to start a conversation, but because we have recognised that the other person does not feel like talking.

If we persist in trying to start a conversation with someone who does not want to talk to us, the person may start to do something else, such as speak with someone else or read a newspaper. They may alternatively tell us that they are very busy, or that they are waiting for someone who is arriving soon. They may even walk away from us. This is the person's way of saying that they really do not want to speak with us at the moment.

Being receptive to conversation

Social interaction is a two-way process. In addition to us wanting to start conversations with other people, it is inevitable that people will want to start conversations with us. It is important to be able to recognise when people would like to speak to us, because to ignore them (even inadvertently) could be considered rude and insulting.

When someone would like to speak with us, they will probably try to make eye contact with us. They may also smile at us or give us an 'eyebrow flash' – this is the person's way of showing that they have seen us and would like to have our attention. In such circumstances, it is appropriate to smile back.

If the person is not already standing or sitting near us, they will probably walk towards us. When they are standing in front of us or to one side, they will perhaps lean slightly towards us or (in more formal circumstances) introduce themselves and shake our hand.

The person will probably ask us a question in order to start a conversation. Alternatively, they may make a statement (such as 'I really like events like this') rather than ask a question. In such cases, they usually expect us to make a suitable response, as if they had added 'don't you?' to the end of their statement.

Choosing the right topic

Having indicated to someone that we would like to speak with them, and hopefully having received some indication that they would like to speak with us, it is now important that we say the right thing. This means finding an appropriate topic of conversation.

There are many possible topics of conversation, and there is no 'right' topic for each particular scenario. The most important thing is to choose a topic that:

- is relevant to the occasion or surroundings

- will put the other person at ease

- is based on something that we and the other person have in common.

When thinking about things to say to start a conversation, think about who you want to talk to, where you are and what is going on. If, for example, you are talking to a friend or family member, you could ask them how work is going or whether they have plans for the weekend. If you are at a conference where you do not know the other person very well, you could ask them about their journey there or whether they enjoyed the lunch.

There are some topics of conversation that can be used on virtually any occasion. Firstly, we can speak about the weather. There is always something happening with the weather, from sun to snow and from fog to floods, and it is something about which everyone has an opinion. It is also completely inoffensive, so makes a great conversation starter. Secondly, we can speak about our surroundings. At a conference or other event, this could include the venue, the food and the speakers. In a more informal setting, this could be the music being played or the number of people present. Thirdly and finally, we can speak about things that we and the other person have in common. If we are at an event in a conference centre, for example, we know that both we and the other person have had to travel there, so we could talk about the journey. Or if we are at someone's birthday party, we could ask the other person how they know the host.

There are also some topics that it is best to avoid, because they could make the other person feel uncomfortable, such as personal information (including age, family and relationships), politics, religion and money.

It may sometimes seem impossible to find an appropriate topic with which to start a conversation. So it is often useful, if we know that we are going to be in a situation where we may wish to speak with people, to think in advance about possible topics of conversation. This means that when we are trying to start a conversation, we can concentrate on making a good impression and making the other person feel comfortable, rather than worrying about what to say.

Summary: starting a conversation

- use eye contact, the 'eyebrow flash' and a smile to make a connection

- do not stand too close to the other person – about one-and-a-half metres is fine

- position yourself to one side of the other person

- greet the other person and ask an introductory question

- watch the other person's body language to gauge their reaction

- if the other person does not want to talk to you, respect their privacy.

Speaking

We speak to people for many reasons. We may wish to communicate information or to find something out, or we may wish to convince someone of our point of view. Whatever the reason for talking to someone, it is not just what we say that is important.

This is because when we speak to someone, it is the overall impression we give that is key – what we say, how we say it and what body language we use while we are speaking.

Consequently, we have to make sure that our body language is consistent with what we are saying. If it is not, we can give mixed messages to the person that we are speaking to, which may reduce the impact of what we are trying to say or even change its meaning completely.

So when we speak to people, we need to pay attention not only to what we say and the tone and pitch of our voice, but also to our facial expressions, our gestures and how we position our bodies. By ensuring that each aspect of our body language is 'in tune' with what we are trying to say, we can make sure that our message comes across loud and clear.

Getting close

When we speak to someone, we first need to be close enough for them to be able to hear us without being so close that we invade their personal space. As when starting a conversation with someone, a distance of about one to one-and-a-half metres should be about right.

We should also avoid standing directly facing someone, as this could be seen as aggressive. The exception to this rule is if we are speaking with someone to whom we are very close, such as a partner or good friend. In such cases, standing directly facing the other person can create a sense of intimacy. In general, however, it is best to stand in front of and slightly to one side of the person we are talking to. This is a more 'open' position, and is likely to make the person we are talking to feel more at ease.

Stand in front, but slightly to one side of other people when speaking to them.

Avoid standing too close to other people, or directly in front of them.

Making a connection

As when starting a conversation, making eye contact with the other person when we are speaking to them is crucial. However, maintaining constant eye contact with someone can make him or her feel uncomfortable, as if they are being interrogated. In order to avoid this, we should make frequent eye contact with the other person, but should only hold this eye contact for a maximum of about seven seconds at a time.

We should make eye contact with the other person in particular when we are starting a new sentence or new thought, or when we are asking a question. When we are not making eye contact, we can look to one side, over the other person's shoulder or down at our desk. We should not, however, look around us to see what else is going on or look to see what other people are doing, as this could make the other person think that we are not interested in talking to them.

Adding emotion and emphasis

We can use our facial expression and head movements to add emotion and emphasis to what we are saying. Our face, in particular, should mirror the tone of what we are saying. For example, if we are telling somebody something exciting (such as 'I just won the lottery' or 'my brother just got a great new job'), we should smile as we speak. If, on the other hand, we are saying something sad or giving someone bad news, we should try to maintain a neutral expression and should definitely not smile.

When speaking to someone, we should keep our head upright, rather than looking at the floor. This will make it easier to make eye contact with the other person and will also help to make us appear confident and outgoing. We should be careful, though, not to tilt our head back and look down at the other person, as they could perceive this to be arrogant or aggressive.

In addition to facial expressions, we can also use head movements to help emphasise what we are saying. If we want to draw attention to key words or points, we can nod our head or lean forward as we say them. This is equivalent to underlining something when we write it, and helps to show that what we are saying is particularly important.

Reinforcing the point

Just as we use facial expressions to add emphasis to what we are saying, we can also use our hands to illustrate our words and to reinforce our message. When we speak, our hands are the equivalent of punctuation marks or bullet points.

We can make a number of gestures with our hands to reinforce what we are saying. As a general rule, however, we should try to keep our hands between waist and shoulder height, otherwise we risk looking frantic or aggressive. We should also try to keep the palms of our hands visible to the person we are speaking to, as this conveys openness and honesty. It is important, however, not to point at people when we are speaking to them, as this can be seen as impolite.

Of the many gestures we can make with our hands when speaking, there are four that are particularly useful. Firstly, we can use our hands to demonstrate two different points of view. For example, we can say 'on the one hand…' and literally display our right hand, and then say 'on the other hand…' and display our left hand. This demonstrates visually that we are explaining two different aspects of something, and can also be used with sentences like 'she says …, but he says …' or 'I agree with you, but we also need to consider…'

Secondly, if we want to present a number of ideas, we can count them on our fingers. For example, we could say 'there could be lots of explanations for her not talking to you. One: she was tired; two: she didn't see you; three: she was distracted and in a hurry…' We can display a closed hand at first and when we come to the first point, we can extend our index finger, at the second point display our middle finger – while also keeping our index finger extended – and so on. This may be a gesture you notice lecturers or speakers using.

Thirdly, we can indicate 'I don't know' by shrugging our shoulders and turning both palms upwards. This gesture can be emphasised further if we shake our head slowly from side to side. While most people will probably understand this gesture even if we do not actually say anything, it can also be used to reinforce sentences such as 'I don't know how it happened' or 'he didn't even give an explanation' – anything where there is an element of not knowing something.

Finally, we can use our hands to show confidence and to convince other people that we know what we are talking about. We can do this by holding our hands in front of us with our palms slightly apart but with our fingertips together, forming a 'steeple' shape – this gesture projects confidence and is often used by business people and politicians. We can use this gesture whether we are standing up or sitting down – in fact, it is particularly effective if we are sitting on a chair resting our hands on the table in front of us. And when we are standing up, it is helpful because it gives us something to do with our hands. If we use this gesture too much, however, we could be seen as over-confident or arrogant. So it is perhaps best to use it only occasionally, such as when making a key point or summarising an idea.

Giving the right signs

While we can use our face, head and hands to add emphasis to what we are saying, we must remember that our arms and feet can also say a lot about what we are thinking and how we are feeling. As people do not generally control consciously what they do with their arms and legs when they are speaking or listening, these can be valuable indicators of what someone really thinks. That is why it is important that what we say with this aspect of our body language matches the words coming out of our mouth.

When we are speaking, we should hold our arms in front of us or at our sides and, as we have discussed, we could use our hands to illustrate what we are saying. What we should try to avoid doing is crossing our arms, as by doing this we are indicating to the person we are speaking to that we are not open to new ideas, that we disagree with them or that we feel defensive.

For the same reason, when we are standing up we should generally avoid crossing our legs or feet. When standing up and speaking to someone, it is best to stand up straight, with our feet slightly apart – this indicates confidence and openness. If we cross our legs or feet, the other person could think that we are nervous or defensive. This could indicate to them that we are not confident in what we are saying or that we do not expect them to believe us, and could reduce significantly the impact of our words. But by having a confident and open stance, we are showing that we believe what we are saying and expect the other person to believe us too.

When we are sitting down, it is perfectly acceptable to cross our legs. When crossing our legs, however, we should try to cross our legs 'towards' the person we are speaking to, to indicate that they have our attention. For example, if the person we are speaking to is seated to our left, we should cross our right leg over our left, so that our right foot is pointing towards the other person. If we were to cross our legs the other way, we would be appearing to 'close ourselves off' from the person we are speaking to.

Adopt a confident and open position when speaking to other people.

Crossing our legs or arms can make people think that we are 'closing ourselves off' from them, or are feeling defensive.

Knowing when to stop

Having looked at how we can use our body language to emphasise and illustrate what we are saying, it is also important to remember that something that interests us may not necessarily be of interest to other people. So it is useful to be able to recognise when someone is not interested in what we are saying, so that we can respond appropriately.

If the person we are talking to is not interested in what we are saying, they will probably make little or no eye contact with us. Instead, they may look around them to see what else is happening or even at the floor. They may cross their arms, and possibly also their legs, indicating that they have closed themselves off from us. They may use oral prompts to move us on to another topic. And they may start to wiggle or tap their feet, showing (possibly subconsciously) that they want to walk away.

If we detect that the person we are speaking to has lost interest in what we are saying, it is important that we do something about it. In most circumstances, the most appropriate thing to do would be to stop speaking and to encourage the other person to speak, perhaps by asking them a question.

Speaking to someone is about more than just talking. We need to make sure not only that we have the other person's attention but also that we use every aspect of our body language – using the techniques that we have discussed here – to reinforce what we are saying. While this may take a bit of effort on our part, it will help to ensure that we communicate what we have to say clearly and effectively.

Summary: speaking

- use body language to reinforce what you are saying

- stand reasonably close to the other person, but not in their personal space

- make frequent eye contact, but only for short periods of time

- use facial expression and head movements to add emotion

- use hand gestures for illustration and expression

- avoid crossing your arms when speaking

- if the other person loses interest, encourage them to speak.

Listening

We have considered the importance of speaking to people clearly and confidently. But it is equally important that we listen to what they have to say. Listening is how we find out what people think, how they feel and why they behave as they do.

However, it is not sufficient just to listen to someone. Listening is an active process – we need to show them that we are listening and be prepared to respond to what they have been saying. If people think that we are not listening to them – even if we are – they can feel that we are not interested in what they have to say. This in turn makes them feel insulted, as if their opinion does not count or, if they are someone close to us, that we don't care about them.

Consequently, when we are listening to someone, we need to let them know that we are listening. We can do this with our body language, for example through our facial expressions and our hand gestures. We can also use certain verbal tactics to show interest and to help us keep track of the conversation.

Giving our full attention

In terms of where we should stand when listening to someone, the same rules apply as when we are speaking to someone. We should aim to be in front of the other person and slightly to one side. If we are listening to someone we know well, for example a partner or good friend, we can stand directly facing him or her to create a sense of closeness. Furthermore, while we should respect the other person's personal space, we can lean slightly towards them from time to time, to indicate that we are listening intently.

In general, we should keep our head, torso and feet facing towards the person we are listening to. This shows that they have our full attention. If we want to show particular interest, we can move one foot forward and point it towards the person we are listening to. This is particularly effective if we are standing in a group of people, and want to show that we are listening to one person in particular.

Looking interested

When people talk to us, they look mainly at our faces to gauge whether or not we are listening to them. Consequently, we should try to keep looking at someone when they are speaking with us. We should avoid closing our eyes, gazing into the middle distance or looking at other things that are going on around us – even though we can still hear what the person is saying to us, they cannot tell that we are listening, and may feel insulted.

In addition to looking towards the person speaking, we should also make frequent eye contact. While we should break this eye contact from time to time, we can comfortably maintain eye contact for longer when we are listening to someone than when we are speaking to them. If looking at the person makes it especially hard for you to hear, or to take information in, you could explain at the beginning of the conversation that, in order to listen carefully, you will need to look away.

It is not just our face and our eyes we can use to show that we are listening – we can use our whole head as well. When we are interested in what someone is saying, we can tilt our head slightly to one side. This shows that we are paying attention to what the

We can show our interest in what other people are saying by looking at them while they speak.

If we look away, they may think that we are not listening to them, or are feeling bored.

person is saying, and can convey to the person speaking that we want them to continue. If we want to encourage them further, we can nod our head from time to time.

We can do this in particular if the person appears nervous or if they make a mistake, as it reassures them that we are interested in what they have to say. And we should, of course, smile at the person speaking – unless they are telling us something serious or sad, in which case we should adopt a neutral expression.

Maintaining focus

When we are listening to someone, it is often tempting to do something else at the same time, such as fiddle with our clothing or tidy our desk. Such behaviour could give the other person the impression that we are not interested in what they have to say or that we have more important things to do. Consequently, we should try to avoid doing anything other than listen to the person who is speaking to us.

We can reassure the other person by keeping our hands at our sides or in front of us, where they are visible. We can also avoid crossing our arms, as the other person could see this as a sign of defensiveness – as if we disagree with them or are not interested in what they are saying.

The person we are listening to should feel that they have our full attention at all times. By concentrating on them and what they are saying, and by using our body language to reinforce this, we can make the person feel more comfortable and more inclined to want to talk to us.

Using verbal tactics to show interest

In addition to using our body language to show that we are listening to someone, there are several verbal techniques that we can use to demonstrate that we have understood what they have told us.

Firstly, we can ask relevant questions to get more information or to ask for clarification. For example, if the person has told us that they went to the cinema at the weekend, we could ask them what film they saw. We should not do this too frequently, though, as it could interrupt the flow of what the person is trying to tell us if we ask questions that do not relate to the main topic of conversation.

Secondly, we can summarise briefly what someone has just said. For instance, if the person has just been telling us about their holiday and all the things they did, we could summarise by saying 'so you didn't just sit on the beach, you went diving and sailing as well'. We can also use this technique to help us remember particular aspects of what the person is telling us, as we are more likely to recall things if we have said them out loud.

Thirdly, we can try to compare what the person has told us with our own experience. This will show the person that we can relate to what they are saying and that we understand their feelings. So if the person has told us that they have just moved to a new job, we could say something like 'I remember when I started my job – I was really nervous'. This can help the person to realise that we and they have something in common, and can encourage them to keep talking freely. However, it is best not to do this too often in one conversation, as it may give the other person the impression that we only want to talk about ourselves.

In using our body language and these verbal techniques, we are not only listening to the person talking to us but we are also showing them that we are listening. By demonstrating to someone that they have our full attention and that we are interested in what they have to say, we can make them feel more comfortable. This can give them a positive impression of us as a 'good listener' and can make them want to talk to us again in the future.

Summary: listening

- listen and let people know that you are listening

- stand close but not in the person's personal space

- direct your head, torso and feet towards the person speaking

- use eye contact to indicate that the person has your attention

- tilt your head to show you are interested and nod to encourage the speaker to continue

- maintain focus – do not do other things or let your attention wander

- use questions, summaries and personal experience to show interest and create a bond.

Having a conversation

A conversation is when two or more people communicate with each other. We have numerous conversations each day – from a quick chat with the newsagent in the morning to a lengthy discussion with friends or family over dinner. Having a conversation with someone is one of the most fundamental forms of human communication, so it is important for us to be able to converse with people confidently.

We have already looked at how we can start a conversation with someone. We have also discussed how we can speak with people and listen to them. Here, we will look at how we can bring all of these together so that we can converse with people easily and effectively. We will also consider specifically two different types of conversation that we are likely to come across on a regular basis – small talk and workplace banter.

Getting the right balance

A conversation should be an interaction between people. When we have a conversation with someone, we want them to feel happy talking to us and to know that we are interested in what they are saying. We will also want to communicate our own views clearly. So it is clear that a conversation will involve both listening and speaking.

The key is to use these two skills in the right proportions. If we speak too much in a conversation, the other person will think that we are rude and that we are not interested in what they have to say. However, if we do not speak enough, they might think that we are not paying attention or that we are not interested in the conversation.

A useful rule for having a conversation is this: we have two ears and one mouth, and should use them in this proportion. This means that we should aim to speak for one third of the time in the conversation and listen for two thirds of the time. Put another way, we should spend twice as much time listening as we do talking.

This might seem a bit odd, because if both people stuck to this rule then, for at least one third of the conversation, nobody would be speaking. That is because this is a rule just for us, not for the other person. Why? Well, when we have a conversation with someone, we want them to enjoy themselves and to feel that we are interested in them and what they are saying. And in general, people like speaking more than they like listening (particularly if they are talking about themselves). So if we let the other person speak for more than half of the time, they are more likely to enjoy the conversation and to think positively about us.

Creating a bond

When we are having a conversation with someone, we should also try to create a bond with him or her. This will help us to communicate with each other more effectively. Such a bond is about more than just the conversation itself, but encompasses every aspect of our relationship with that person.

The bond that we can build up with the person we are talking to will influence how effectively we are able to communicate with them. Therefore, we should do everything we can to establish a strong bond whenever we have a conversation with someone. One way in which we can create a bond is through body language.

Mirroring

When we are having a conversation with someone, we should look at how they use their own body language. Some people use a lot of hand and arm gestures when speaking, for example, while others may stand in a particular way or put their weight on one foot rather than the other.

One way of creating a bond with someone is to 'mirror' the other person's body language, such as their facial expressions, their head movements, their gestures and their posture. For example, if the person we are speaking to is standing in a particular way (perhaps they are standing at a bar with one arm resting on the counter and the other hand in their pocket) or makes particular gestures when speaking (such as holding their hands in front of them with the fingertips of each hand touching), we could adopt a similar position or replicate the gestures when speaking with them.

This mirroring of their gestures or posture makes the other person feel more comfortable when talking with us, as it gives them the impression that we are the same as them. This technique is, therefore, particularly useful when we want to create a bond with someone. We should be careful, however, not to mirror the other person's body language too obviously, because they might think that we are making fun of them. It is usually best to mirror only the person's posture at first (ie how they are standing or sitting) and to mirror some other aspects of their body language from time to time only after we have been speaking with them for a little while.

Note that women's gestures and postures may be different to men's. For example, men and women often sit in different ways. Therefore, it might look out of place if a man were to mirror a woman's posture, or vice versa. In general, though, if the other person's body language is open, friendly and relaxed, it helps if ours is, too.

Synchronising

When we are having a conversation with someone, it is often difficult to know when they are about to stop talking or when they would like to speak. This can result in both people speaking at the same time, or in one person not being able to speak when they would like to.

However, people often use their body language to indicate when they are about to stop talking or when they would like to speak. By observing this body language and by using it ourselves, we can 'synchronise' the conversation so that it flows more smoothly.

When someone is speaking, they will often make frequent eye contact and use hand gestures. When they have finished speaking, they will generally stop making hand gestures and will make eye contact with us, as they expect us to reply. So when the person we are speaking to stops talking, stops making hand gestures and makes eye contact with us, this is usually an indication that they have finished what they want to say. We can, therefore, start to speak without worrying about interrupting them.

If the other person is speaking and we would like to say something, it can seem rude for us to simply start talking while they are still speaking. However, we can indicate that we would like to speak by making eye contact with the other person and saying something like 'yes…' or 'but…'. The person will then hopefully finish what they are saying and wait for our response. Equally, if we are speaking and the other person makes eye contact with us and says something like 'well…' or 'hmm…', we know that they would like to speak. At this point, it would be polite to finish what we are saying and to allow the other person to respond.

Making small talk

One of the most common forms of conversation is known as 'small talk'. Such conversations are usually vague, inconsequential chats between two or more people who find themselves in the same place at the same time. However, the ability to 'make small talk' has significance far out of proportion to the actual conversations themselves.

People are often uncomfortable sitting or standing together in silence, for example at a bus stop or in a dentist's waiting room, so they will engage in small talk on topics such as the weather, items in the news or the latest goings on in the locality. Such conversations are purely a way of passing the time, and are not an attempt by the people involved in them to discuss or resolve any particular issue. In fact, small talk conversations can often ramble across a number of topics without any clear points being made or conclusions being drawn.

Small talk is also often an important part of the work environment. People who work in the same office, for example, may enjoy making small talk as it is a way for them to speak to colleagues and be sociable without being unduly distracted from their work. It can also help the staff team to 'bond'.

Engaging in small talk is an excellent way to practise our communication skills, as the verbal content is generally not very demanding and we can, therefore, concentrate on observing and practising body language techniques. We should not try to make any particular argument, but should just follow the flow of the conversation and encourage the other participants in the conversation to speak.

Participating in workplace banter

Workplace banter is a form of small talk that takes place between work colleagues, particularly those who share an open plan office or work area. Such banter is a light-hearted group conversation in which people can participate while they work. Workplace banter is not usually an ongoing conversation, but rather takes place as a series of 'bursts' of conversation throughout the day. Such conversations can start for any number of reasons, such as in response to something that was on television the previous night or as a result of an email that someone has received.

Workplace banter is different from a typical conversation and as such has a slightly different set of rules. We do not have to stop what we are doing in order to engage in the conversation and do not have to position ourselves in close proximity to or facing the person speaking. In fact, it is usual for all people engaging in such banter to remain at their desks or work stations – and, indeed, to continue with their work – while participating in the conversation.

The key thing is to show awareness of the conversation. If people are smiling or laughing, for example, then we should do the same. If we show no reaction to the conversation, people may think that we are not interested in what they are saying or even that we are being rude. While workplace banter, like small talk, is itself of little consequence, it is a great way to develop good working relationships with our colleagues and to make us 'one of the team'.

We can also use certain aspects of body language to help us engage in workplace banter. When we speak, we can get our colleagues' attention by raising our head from our work. And when listening, we can smile and glance at the person speaking so that they know we are interested. Furthermore, if someone says something funny and everybody laughs out loud, we can share in this moment by laughing as well and looking around at our colleagues.

Small talk and workplace banter can be difficult to master at first, but with practice can become enjoyable ways of learning about people, practising our communication skills and passing a spare few minutes.

Summary: having a conversation

- achieve the right balance between speaking and listening

- encourage other people to speak

- mirror other people's body language to create a bond

- observe and use body language to keep the conversation flowing smoothly

- engage in small talk and workplace banter to pass the time.

Talking with a group of people

Many conversations involve just two people. However, some conversations can take place among a group of three or more individuals. This is often the case at parties or other events, where people will automatically cluster together in small groups.

The basic principles of conversation that we have considered previously apply equally to conversations with groups of people. Some of the key things that we have discussed are:

- stand close to the other person, but not in their personal space

- make frequent eye contact

- try to get the right balance between speaking and listening

- when speaking, use body language to add emotion and to reinforce what we are saying

- when listening, maintain focus and pay attention to what the other person is saying

- show that we are listening by maintaining eye contact and tilting our head slightly

- encourage the other person to continue speaking by nodding or using verbal techniques to show interest

- mirror the other person's body language to create a bond.

However, there are some additional considerations that we should

bear in mind when joining, participating in and leaving group conversations.

Joining a group conversation

When thinking about whether or not to join a particular group, we can use the group's body language to see if we are likely to be accepted into the conversation.

If two people are having a conversation, they may be standing close together and facing each other directly. In this case, the people are probably having a personal conversation and it would be inappropriate to join them. If, on the other hand, the people are standing in a more 'open' position at an angle to each other, they may be receptive to us joining them. If we wish to, we could try to join this conversation. However, if the people turn to face each other when we approach them, this is a sign that our interruption is not welcome.

Where three or more people are having a conversation, the group has already been established and is much more likely to welcome us into its discussion. It is, therefore, much easier for us to join a larger group, particularly if we are not confident in our ability to read people's body language.

Having decided to join the group, it is easiest to position ourselves on the edge of the group, facing the person speaking. If the group is happy for us to join the conversation, the people in the group will generally make room for us and angle their bodies a little towards us to include us in the conversation. They may also make eye contact with us and perhaps nod or use an 'eyebrow flash'. If the other people do not make room for us, or if they acknowledge us only by looking at us briefly and then turning away, then this is a sign that we are not welcome in the group.

When we have joined a group, we can think about getting involved in the conversation. We can start by listening to the person who is speaking at the time, and can make eye contact with them, nod and use other body language to show we are listening. We should definitely spend some time getting used to the topic, nature and flow of the conversation before we try to say anything ourselves.

Knowing when to speak

As the person speaking is finishing what they have to say, they will probably stop making hand gestures and then stop speaking. At this point, however, there may be a number of people within the group who want to speak next.

If we want to speak, we should wait until the person currently speaking is finishing – we can generally tell this either from their body language or from the context of what they are saying. At this point, we can indicate our wish to speak by making a conspicuous hand gesture (for example, we could hold out one hand as if illustrating a particular point) and making eye contact with the person speaking. Once the person has finished speaking, we can start to talk. If at this point someone else starts to speak as well, it is polite to let him or her continue, by saying something like 'sorry, you first'. When that person has finished speaking, people will generally then look at us and wait for us to speak. Alternatively, people may say something like 'after you', to indicate that they are happy for us to speak first.

Speaking to a group

When speaking to a group of people, it can be difficult to know where to look. We can start by making eye contact with the person who has just finished speaking, but should try to make eye contact with as many people in the group as possible. Rather than just move our eyes around the group in a circle, it is often more effective to make brief eye contact (ie a few seconds) with people in the group at random. This helps to make everyone in the group feel included in the conversation.

When speaking to the group, we should be aware that other people may also wish to speak. We should, therefore, keep our contributions short and to the point. We should also try to watch the body language of the people in the group, so that we can tell if they would also like to speak.

If people in the group make conspicuous hand gestures or say things like 'well…' or 'but…' as we are speaking, particularly as we reach the end of a sentence, this is an indication that they would like to speak. If this happens, we should finish the point we are making and then make eye contact with them to let them know that we have finished. Even if no one else looks as if they would like to speak, we should not speak for more than a few minutes at the most, or people may think that we are trying to dominate the discussion.

Leaving a group

When we leave a group conversation, particularly if we have been involved in the discussion, it is polite to let people know that we are leaving. If the group is large, we can just wave briefly at the group in general and then step away. If the group is small, we can wait for a break in the conversation and then say goodbye. When saying goodbye, we could also tell the people within the group that it has been nice speaking to them.

Conversations with a group can be more difficult than conversations with one other person, because there are more people involved and more things to which we need to pay attention. They can also be easier, because there is less pressure on us to participate all of the time. Group conversations do, however, present us with the opportunity to communicate with a large number of people at once, so it is well worth practising the skills that we need to engage in them effectively.

Summary: talking with a group of people

- observe people's body language to decide whether it is appropriate to join a particular group

- join the edge of a group and wait for it to accept you

- recognise that many people in the group may wish to speak

- when speaking, make eye contact with as many people in the group as possible

- do not speak for too long

- watch people's body language to see if they want to speak

- wave or say goodbye when leaving the group.

Social events

Social events come in all shapes and sizes, ranging from a small party in someone's living room to an industry conference in a giant exhibition hall. All involve people, noise, lights and – more often than not – a fair amount of chaos. At best, social events are daunting. At worst, they can be terrifying.

Such events are, however, nothing more than lots of groups of people engaging in conversation. By using the skills and techniques that we have discussed so far, we can not only cope with social events, but perhaps even enjoy them.

Planning for the event

The good thing about any particular social event is that it has a specific purpose. For example, it may be to celebrate someone's birthday, to allow a company's employees to relax at the end of a tough year or to bring together representatives from a particular industry or profession.

This means that everybody at a particular social event automatically has something in common. For example, people going to someone's birthday party will all know the host, and many will probably know each other. People attending a conference will all work in the same field or at least have a shared interest.

By thinking about the nature of the social event, we can get a good idea of who will be there and what we will have in common with them. This will, in turn, help us to think about the sort of situations we are likely to encounter and give us some ideas for potential topics of conversation. So when we attend the event, we can spend our time interacting with people rather than worrying about what we should do and what we should say.

Understanding groups and 'mingling'

At any social event, people will tend to gather into groups. Groups will form in particular around places where there is food or drink, where there is somewhere to sit or where there is some kind of focal point (such as a table or other piece of furniture).

Groups at social events are generally open to newcomers to join them. We can join such groups and engage in conversation using the techniques that we have already discussed.

However, it is common at social events for people to move from group to group relatively quickly, spending only a few minutes interacting with each. This practice is called 'mingling', and is an effective way of meeting as many people as possible in a limited period of time, particularly if you are the host.

Mingling can be quite tiring, because it involves joining, interacting with and leaving a number of groups in quick succession. If we want to meet as many people as possible, or if we are the host of the event, then interacting with each group in turn may be desirable or (in the case of the host) expected. Otherwise, we may find it less stressful to interact with two or three groups briefly at first and then find a group in which we feel comfortable to 'settle down' for the rest of the event, or at least for a longer period of time.

The idea of interacting with different people at a social event may at first appear rather intimidating. However, it is useful to remember that most people are a little anxious about social occasions and meeting new people. If we are confident, positive and use appropriate body language, people will usually be only too happy to engage in conversation with us.

Leaving the event

Just as it is polite to say goodbye when leaving a group, it is courteous to say goodbye before leaving an event. For smaller events, we may be able to say goodbye to everybody there. In particular, however, we should say goodbye to the host and compliment them on their hospitality.

At larger events where it is not practical to say goodbye to everybody, we may wish to say goodbye to people with whom we have spent a significant amount of time during the event, to anybody we are likely to meet again afterwards, and to any close friends or colleagues who are there.

It may seem easier to just leave the event without saying goodbye. However, this may result in people not knowing whether we are still at the event or not, and they could worry if they are unable to find us. Saying goodbye to people when we leave the event can also make them feel flattered, because we have taken the trouble to come and find them before leaving. This means that, even when we are no longer at the event, we have left a positive impression.

Summary: social events

- remember that social events are just lots of individual conversations

- learn about the event and think about who will be there

- plan what you will do and what you can talk about

- feel free to move from group to group

- if things get stressful, find a group where you can settle down

- do not forget to say goodbye before you leave.

In case of emergency

No matter how much we practise our body language, there will always be some social situations in which we are not sure what to do. This happens to everybody at some point, and the important thing is not to panic.

By taking things slowly and focusing on the basics of body language, we can communicate effectively with people in virtually all circumstances.

Getting time to think

When we are in a busy social or work environment, we will sometimes not want to interact with people straight away. We may want a bit of time to ourselves or we may want to get used to the environment before starting to talk to people. And sometimes we may just not want any social contact at all.

There are a number of ways in which we can show people that we need to be left alone, which will give us some time to think without making other people think we are being rude.

The best thing to do if we need a bit of time to ourselves is to look as if we are very busy, as this will usually stop people from interrupting us. There are a number of ways we can do this. Firstly, we can pretend to be reading something, such as a bus timetable, a newspaper or a leaflet. Secondly, if we have a mobile phone then we can pretend that we are sending a text message to someone. All we have to do is put the keypad lock on our phone and then tap away. Thirdly, we can pretend to be writing something, as if we need to write down some ideas before we forget them. We can also go to the toilet – if only to wash our hands and have a couple of minutes to ourselves.

Any of these techniques will only work for a few minutes. However, they will give us valuable time to think about the environment we are in and how we can interact with the people in it.

Going back to basics

Sometimes we will want to interact with another person but will not know what to do. However, in any social situation where we are not sure how to interact with the other person or what body language to use, there are a number of basic things that we can do to establish a basis for communication with that person. This will give us more time to think about what to do.

1 Make eye contact

We have seen that eye contact forms the basis of all non-verbal communication. Making eye contact shows that we have noticed that the other person is there and that we are prepared to communicate with them.

2 Acknowledge the other person

Having made eye contact with the person, we should acknowledge them with a smile and with appropriate gestures or words. For example, we could nod our head or use an 'eyebrow flash'. If the person is near to us, we could simply say 'hello'.

3 Adopt a non-threatening stance

When interacting with someone, we should make sure that we are not standing in their personal space. In practice, this means that we should be standing at least a metre to a metre-and-a-half away from them. To reinforce the message that we are not aggressive, we should make sure that the person can see the palms of our hands. We can do this by holding our arms at our sides with our palms open and relaxed, possibly facing slightly forwards – there is no need to have your palms facing directly towards the other person, as this is likely to be physically uncomfortable.

4 Observe the other person

By listening to the other person and observing their body language, we will be able to gain information on what they want and how we should respond. We can also consider the interaction in the context of what is happening around us. For example, if we are visiting someone's office and they are walking towards us with their hand outstretched, it is likely that they are coming to greet us and want to shake our hand. Or if we are standing at a bus stop and the person next to us has turned towards us and asked a question, it is likely that they want to start a conversation with us or engage in small talk.

5 Respond positively and confidently

Once we have identified the nature of the interaction, we are in a better position to respond appropriately. In all cases, we should try to create a good impression by responding positively and confidently using both verbal and non-verbal communication.

Overcoming difficulty making eye contact

We have considered the importance of eye contact in many social interactions. However, sometimes we may not feel comfortable making eye contact with people. To me, for example, it can often feel as if their eyes are like lasers probing into my brain.

If this is the case, we can make eye contact by looking not into the person's eyes, but at the gap between their eyes, towards the top of their nose. The person we are looking at will not be able to tell the difference, and it can make us feel a lot more comfortable.

Avoiding people without causing offence

On some occasions, somebody may be talking to us but we just want them to leave us alone. This may be because we are tired and need some time alone or because we do not particularly like the other person. However, to just walk away from them would be seen as very rude.

There are, however, ways in which we can politely end the conversation with the other person. How we do this depends on whether we wish to stay in the room we are in or the event that we are at and talk to someone else (for example, at a party) or if we are planning to leave.

If we plan to stay but want to talk to someone else, there are a number of things that we can do. Most easily, we can finish what we are saying, make eye contact with the person and say something like 'Well, it was good to see you; enjoy the rest of the evening', before smiling and walking away from them. This is the easiest way of ending the conversation, but not the most subtle way.

We can be more subtle about ending a conversation by giving the other person a reason why we have to stop talking with them. For example, we could say that we have just seen someone to whom we need to speak urgently, or that we want to speak with someone whom we know will be going home soon, so have to catch them quickly. Or if we are at an event where there is food and drink provided, we could say that we are going to get something to eat.

The most polite thing to do if we want to end a conversation is to introduce the person with whom we are talking to someone else, and to then leave the two of them talking to each other. This can be quite difficult, though, particularly if we do not know many of the people present.

If we wish to leave the event, it is a little easier to end a conversation. In such circumstances, we can simply look at our watch and say something like 'Oh, is that the time? I'd better get going.' We can then say goodbye to the person we are talking to and leave without causing them any offence.

Summary: in case of emergency

- if you need some time alone, pretend to be reading, writing or using your mobile phone

- focus on the body language basics: eye contact, a smile and a non-threatening stance

- observe other people's body language and what is happening around you

- respond to people positively and confidently using verbal and non-verbal communication

- if you are uncomfortable making eye contact with someone, focus instead on the gap between their eyes

- to end a conversation with someone, be polite and explain why you have to move on.

Developing our body language skills

Learning body language is like learning any other language. We do not master it all at once, but develop our skills slowly over time. There are three main ways in which we can develop our body language skills. Firstly, we can practise them, either on our own or in social environments. Secondly, we can watch how other people use body language and learn from them. And finally, we can make use of books and other resources.

Practising body language

The best way to practise body language is with real people in real social environments. However, this can be quite daunting, particularly if we are not completely confident in our skills.

We can start by practising in front of a mirror. This is particularly useful for practising things like eye contact, facial expressions and hand gestures. We can also practise things like handshakes and conversations with people we trust, who can give us feedback on how our body language comes across.

Once we are confident in the basic aspects of body language, we can try them out in familiar social environments, such as with family and friends. By practising with people we know, it is not a problem if we make mistakes at first. These people can also help us to develop our body language by letting us know if we do something inappropriate.

When we have tried out our skills on our family and friends, we can practise them in other social environments, such as at

school, college or university, at work or when out shopping. This
will mean that we experience a variety of environments, and
have the opportunity to practise our skills in a range of different
interactions.

Learning from other people

We can also develop our body language by watching other people.
For example, we can watch other people's body language when they
are talking to us. We can look at their facial expressions, what they
do with their hands and how they stand. We can also try to relate
their body language to the words that they are using, so that we get
a good idea of how people's body language changes depending on
their mood, what they are saying and who they are with.

We can also observe people in different environments, for example
when they are socialising in groups or when they are arguing
with each other. One of the best ways to do this is to sit in the
window of a coffee shop in a busy area of town and watch what is
happening outside. However, people can feel uncomfortable if they
think that they are being watched, so it is best not to watch any
single person for more than a few minutes.

A final way to learn from other people's body language is to watch
them when they are on television. Actors are trained to use body
language to communicate and to show their emotions, so the
characters in films and soap operas can be a useful source of facial
expressions, gestures and other aspects of body language. Politicians
are also well-versed in using body language to complement what
they are trying to say, so watching them on the news and in

documentaries can be very useful. A further helpful source of body language is chat shows, where the host interviews celebrities or ordinary members of the public. By watching such programmes, we can see how people react when questioned and how their body language changes when they are happy or sad, confident or defensive.

Useful books and resources

Another useful way to learn more about body language, and in particular about how to read other people's body language, is from books and other resources.

There are a number of books devoted to body language, which are available from most large bookshops. A couple that I have found useful are:

- *Body language* by Gordon Wainwright. Published by Teach Yourself.

- *The definitive book of body language* by Allan and Barbara Pease. Published by Orion Books.

There are, however, many more books available. It can also be useful to look in your bookshop's business management section, where there are likely to be lots of books on skills such as negotiation, sales and coaching. These can give valuable hints on how to act in specific situations, such as when we are working in a team or when we are speaking to a large group of people.

In addition to books, there are also many websites devoted to body language. These range from sites promoting books and consultants to those about particular aspects of body language (such as knowing when someone is lying), and to online dictionaries of all sorts of facial expressions, hand gestures and other elements of non-verbal behaviour. A quick search of the internet can give you an idea of what is available, though you will inevitably find some sites more useful than others.

And finally...

Developing and using body language as a way of communicating with people can be a complicated, nerve-racking and – occasionally – uncomfortable experience. However, each time we get out and interact with people, we will improve. This means that the more we practise, the easier we will find it to develop relationships with people and to communicate effectively.

Whatever your aim in reading this book, I hope you have found what you are looking for. I hope that I have been able to share with you my own enthusiasm for body language as a way of breaking down the barriers between people. And I hope that I have convinced you that we can use body language to communicate more successfully and more enjoyably with our families, our friends and all the other people in our lives.